# THIS BOOK BELONGS TO

....................................................................

....................................................................

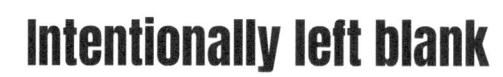
Intentionally left blank

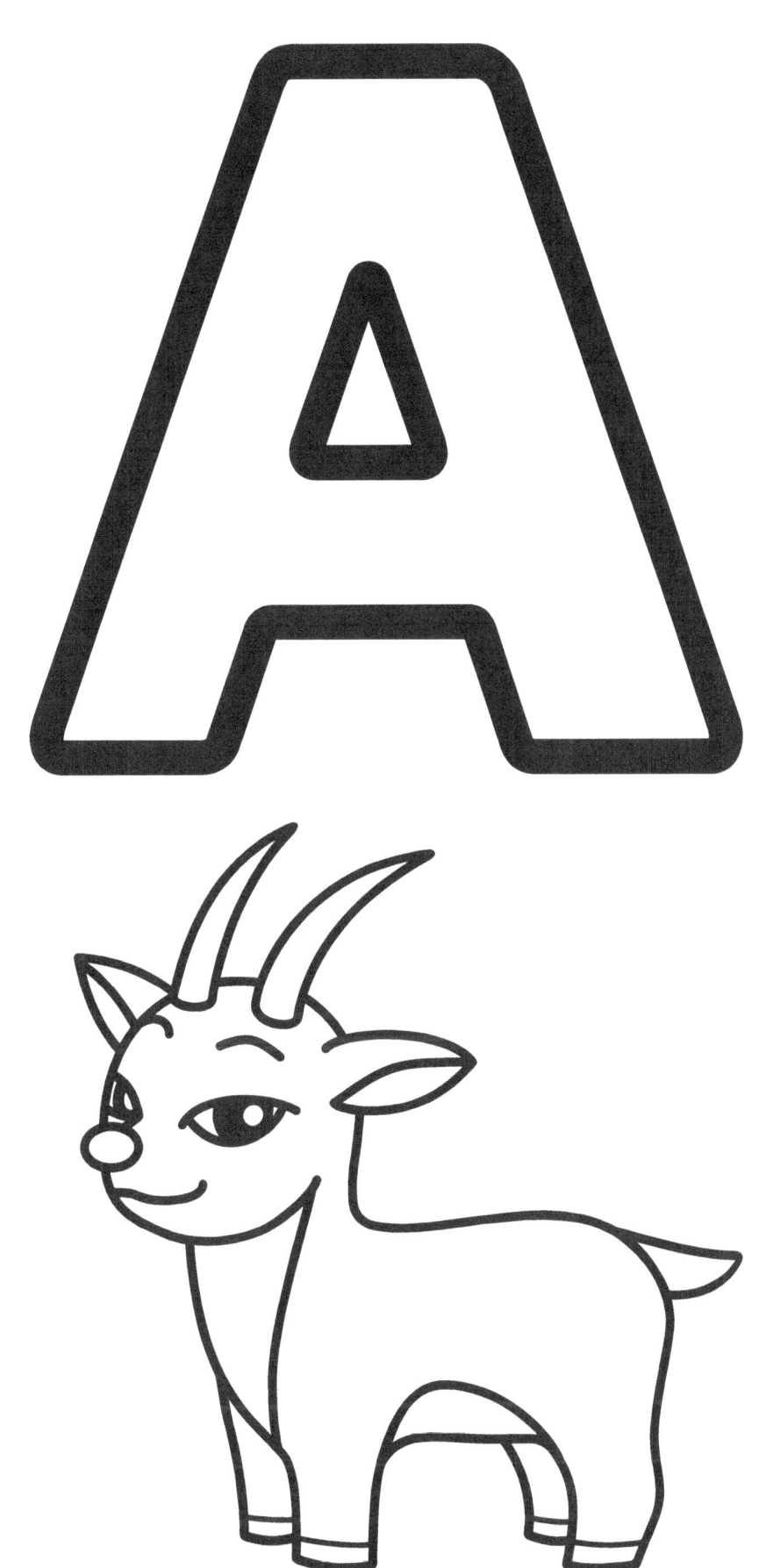

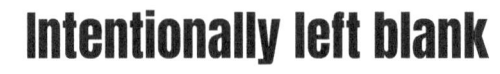
Intentionally left blank

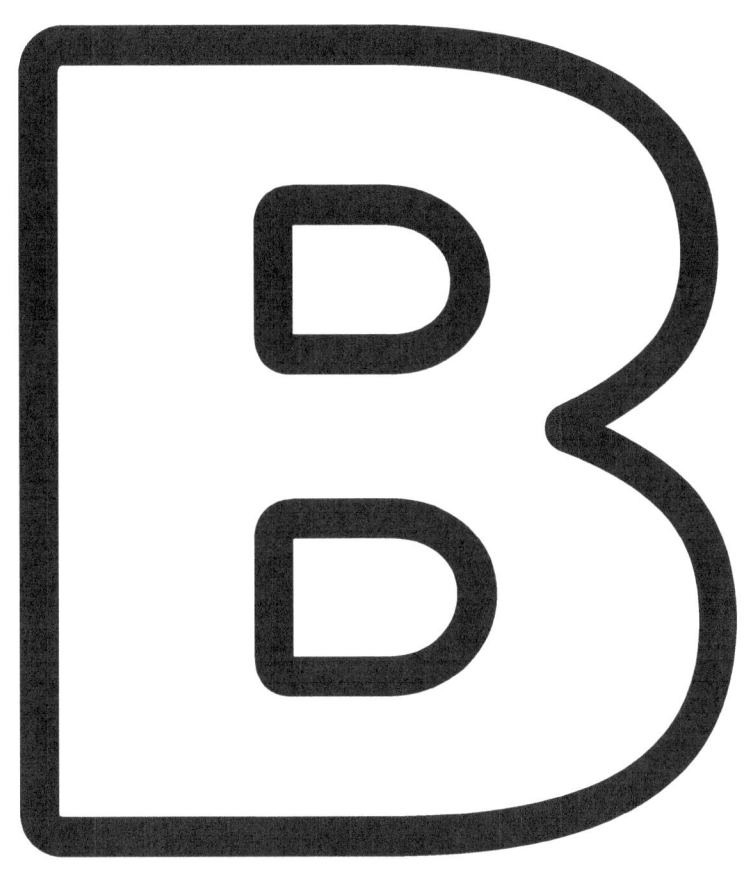

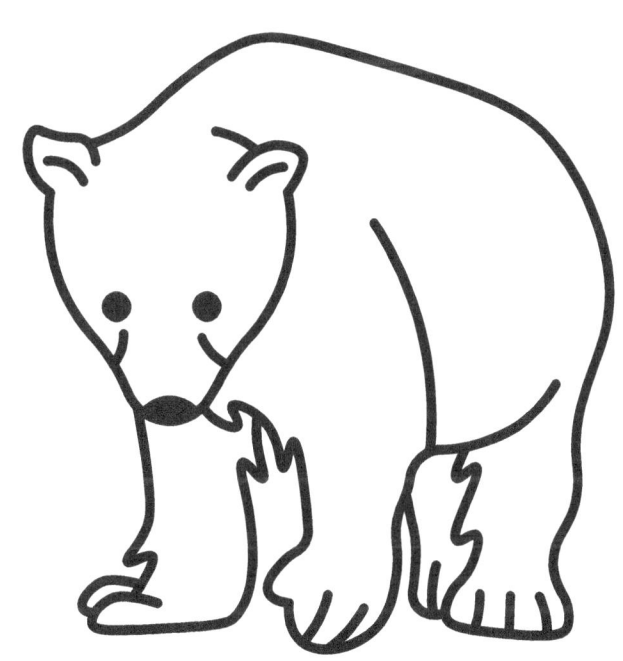

Intentionally left blank

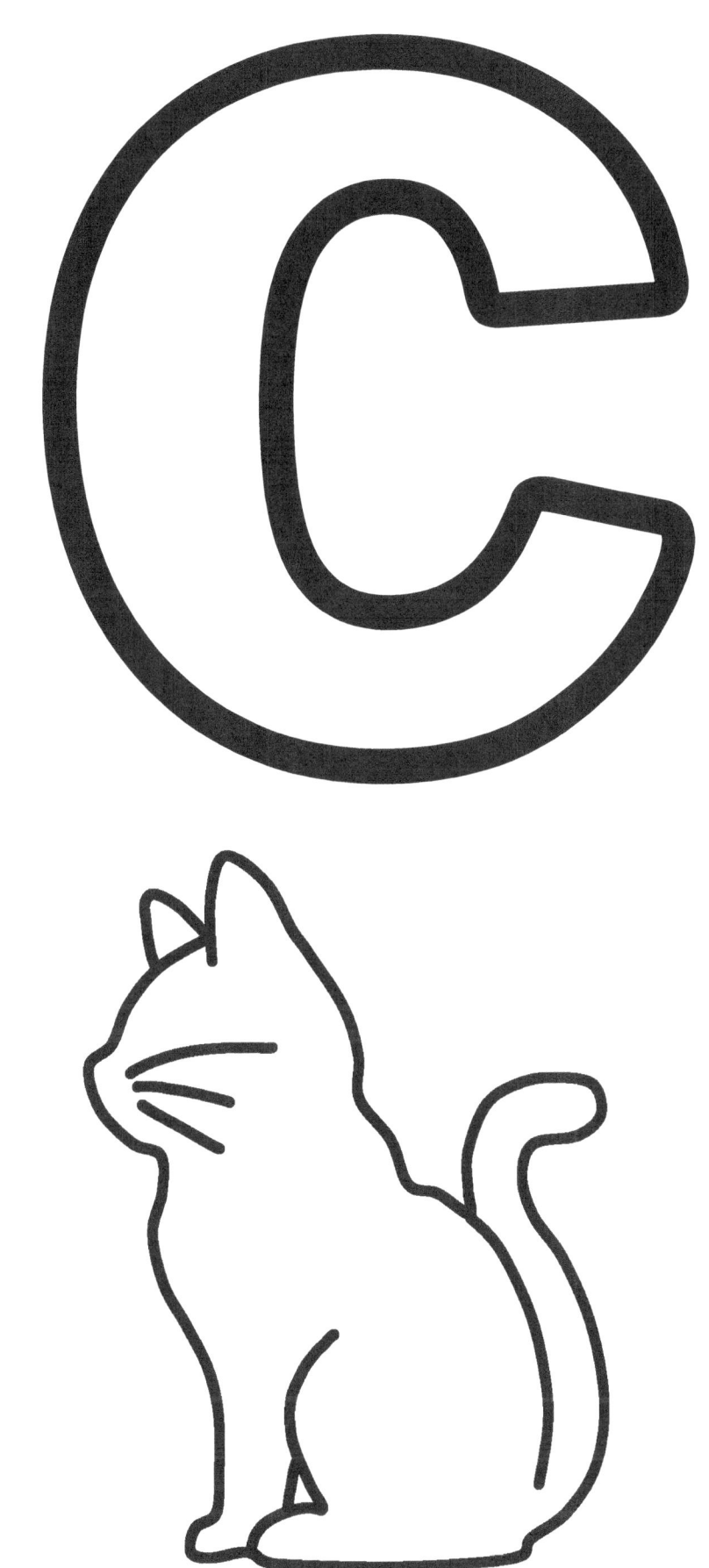

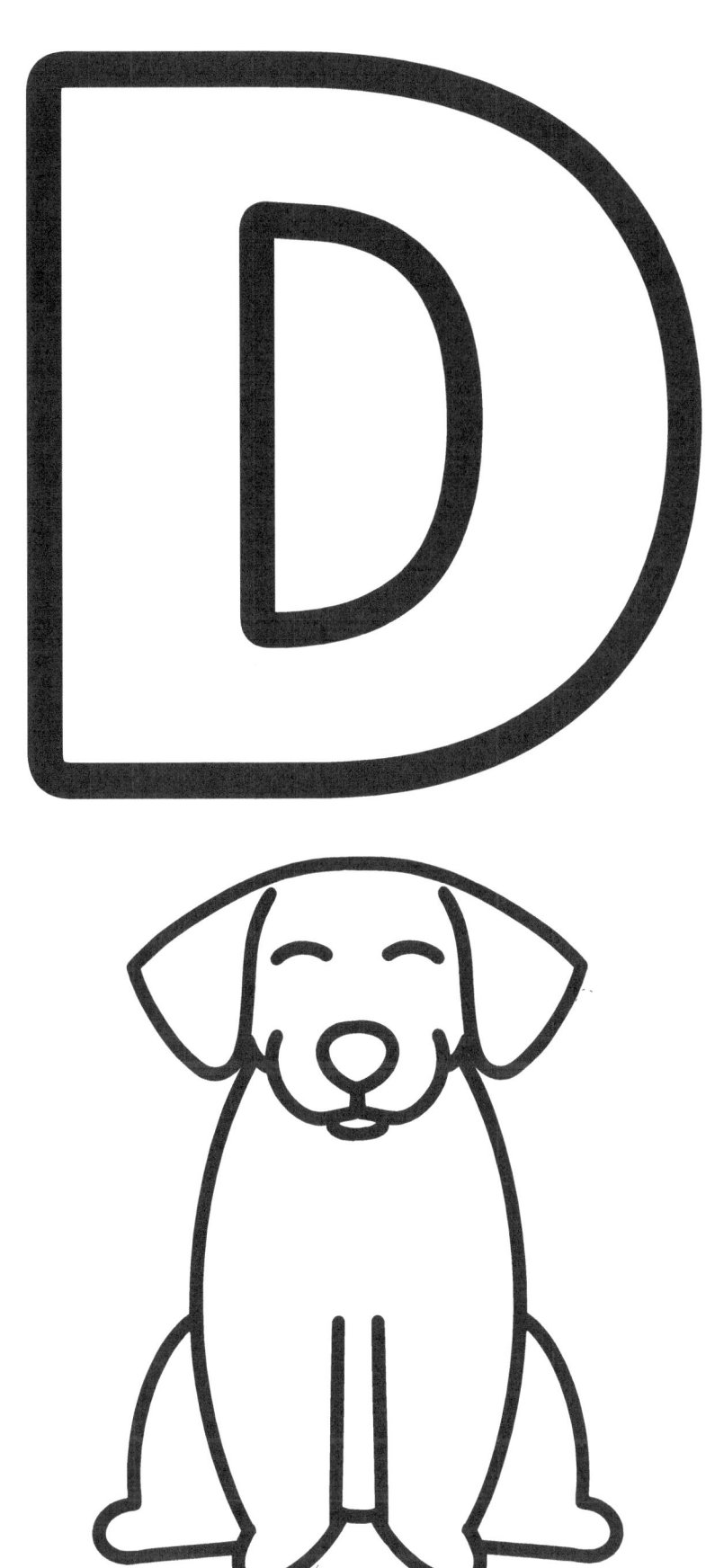

Intentionally left blank

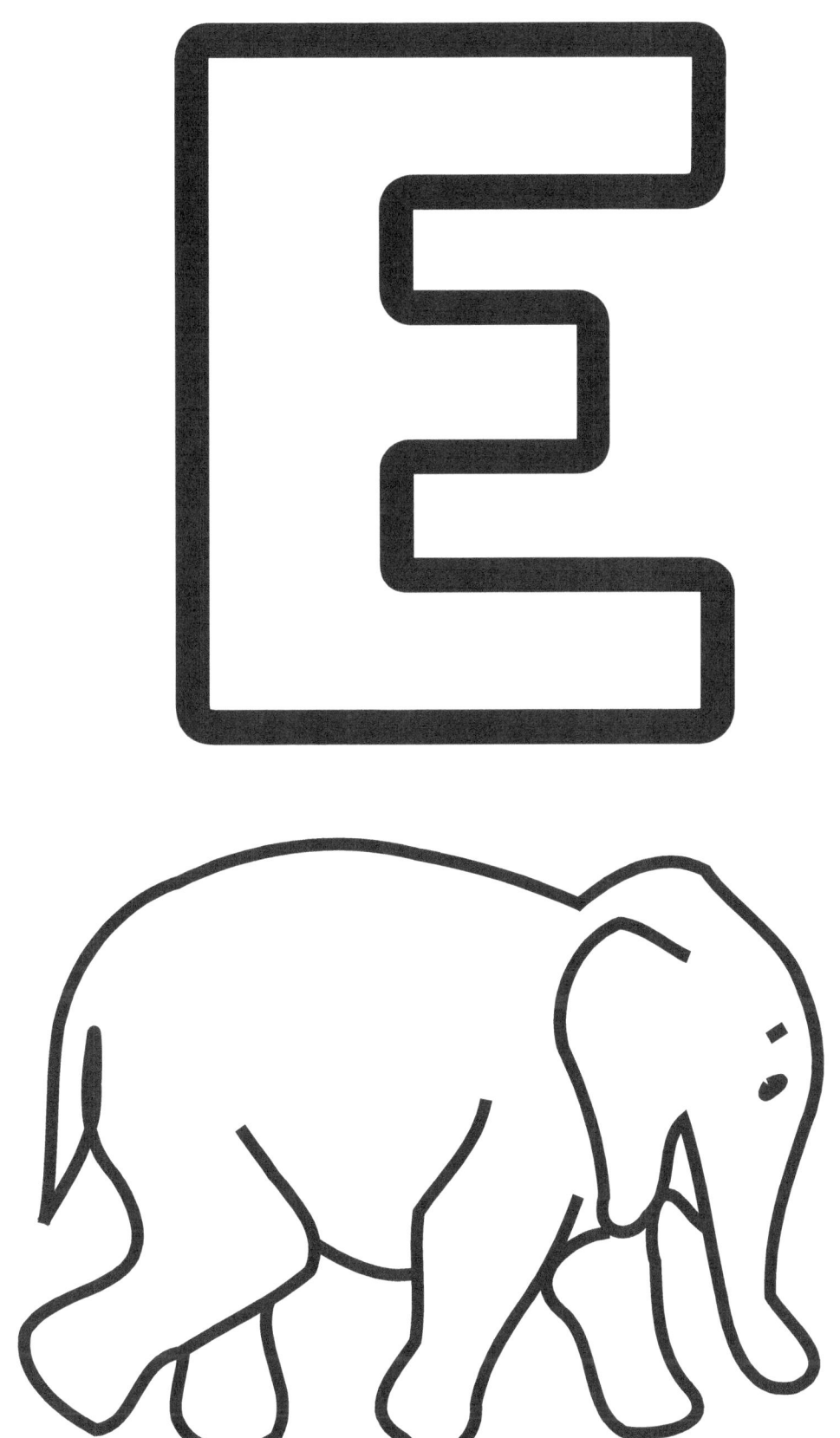

Intentionally left blank

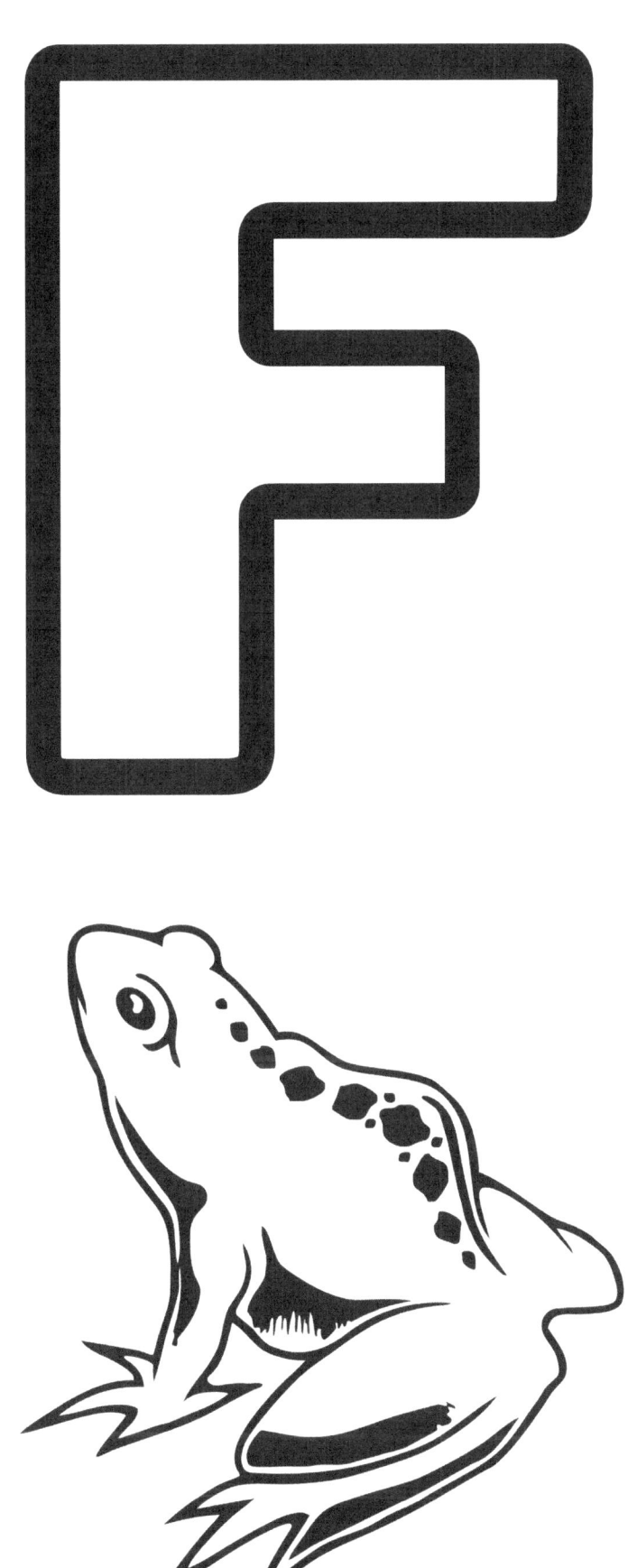

Intentionally left blank

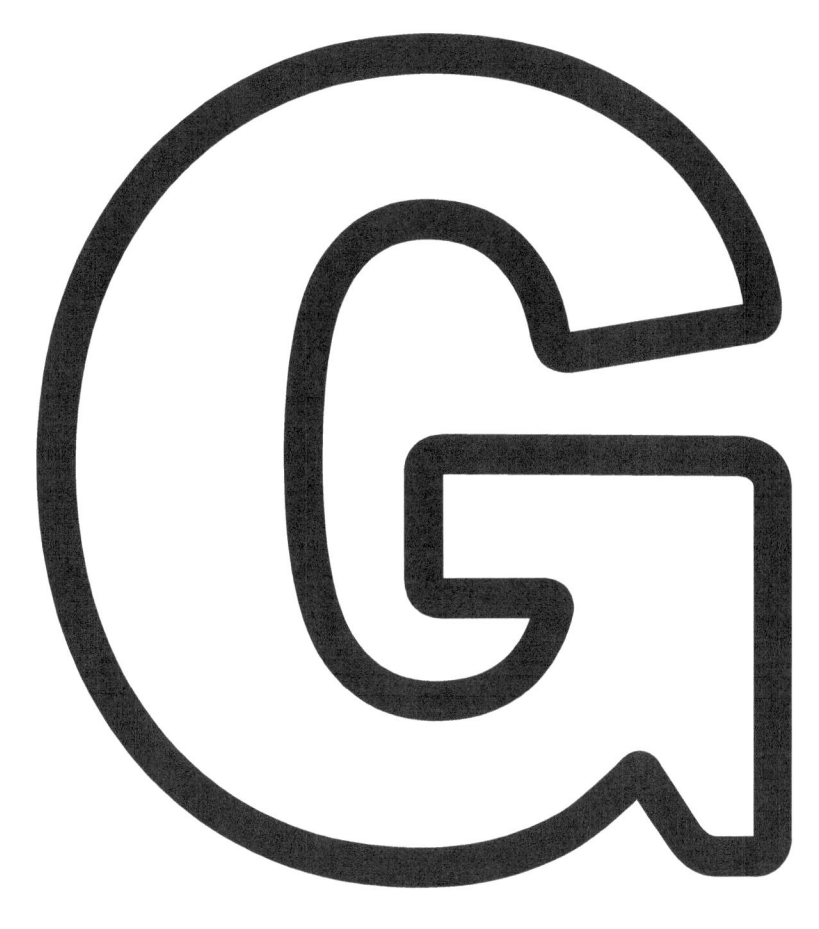

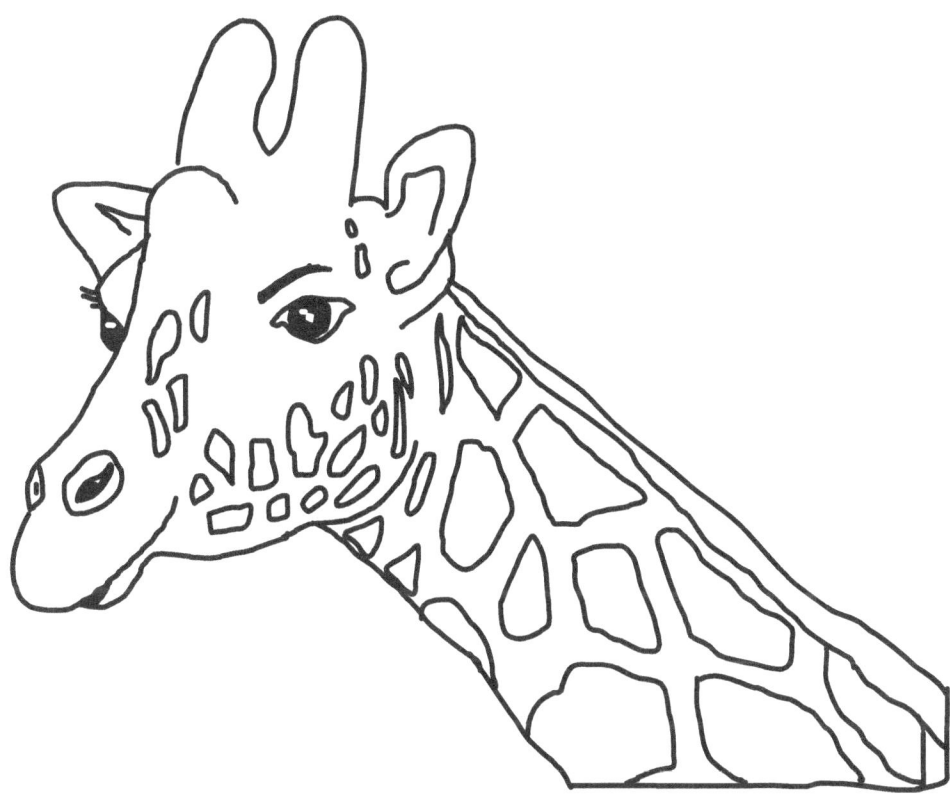

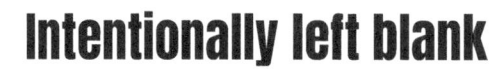
Intentionally left blank

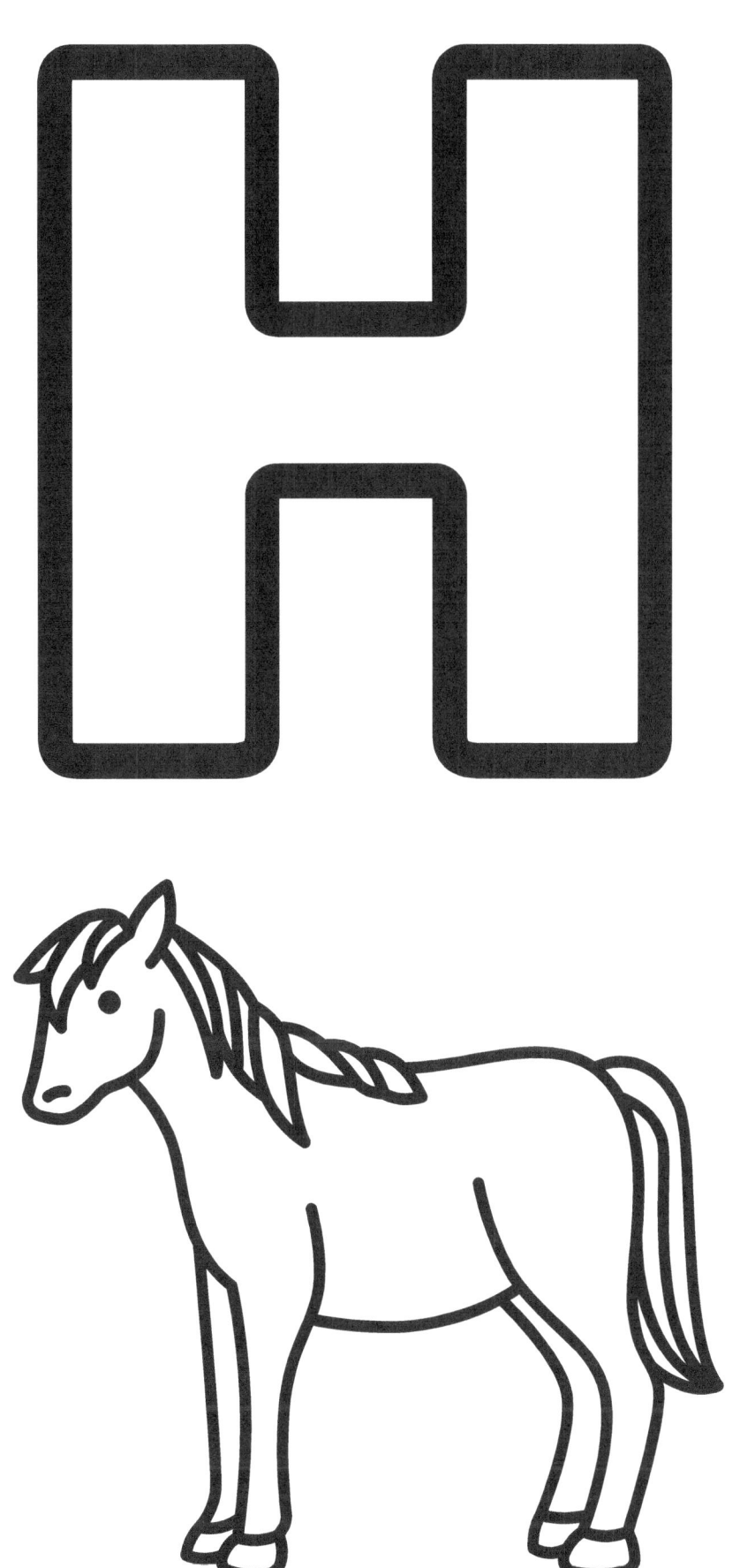

Intentionally left blank

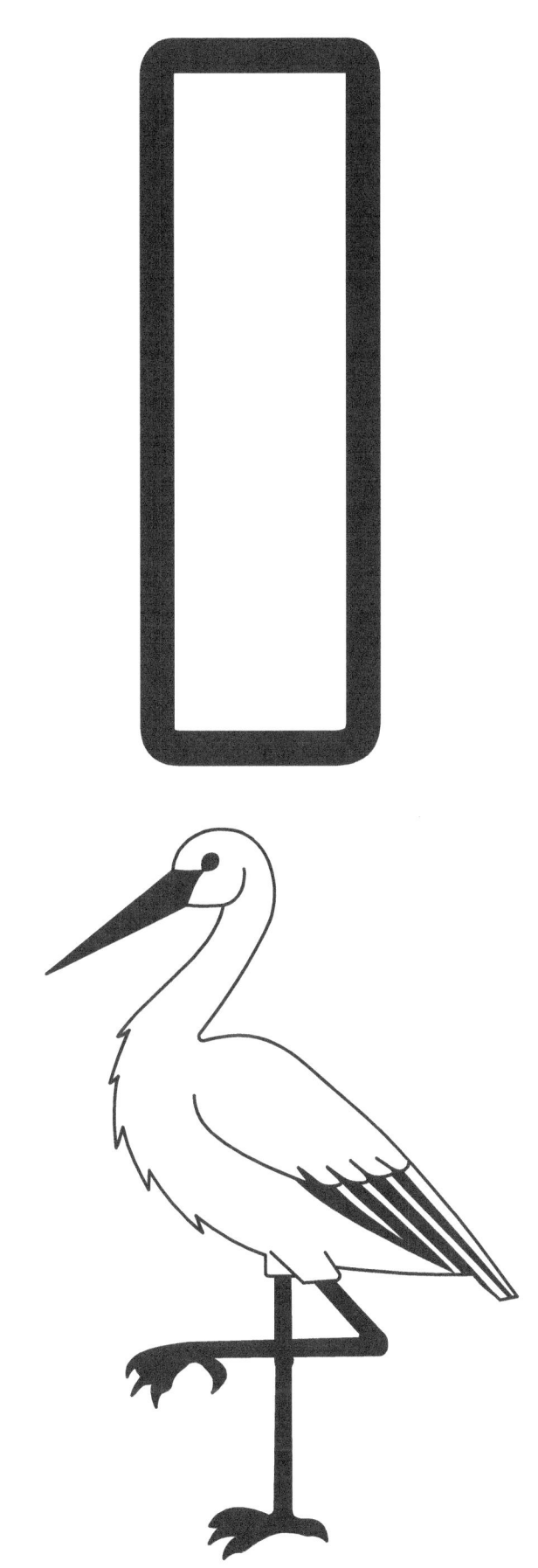

Intentionally left blank

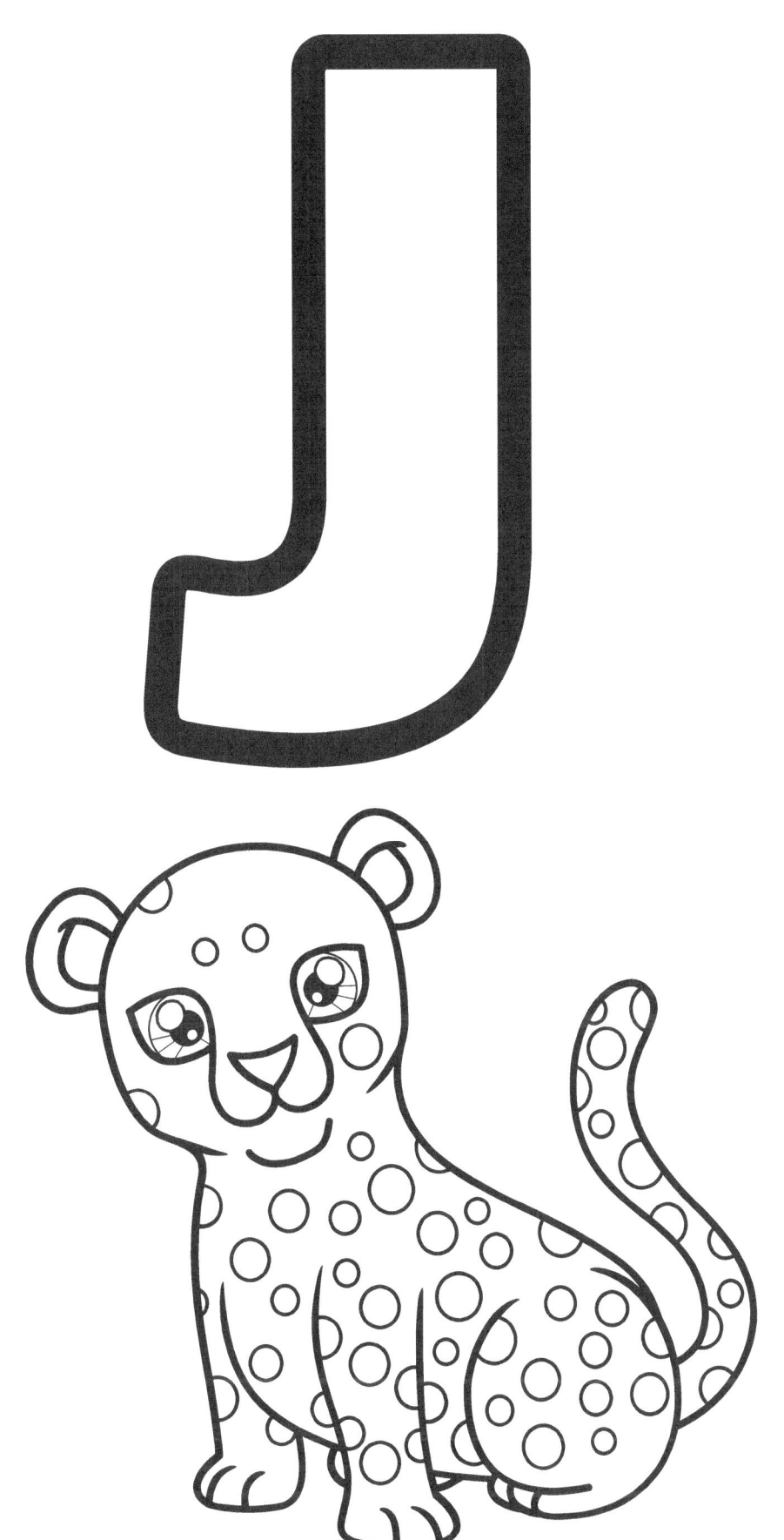

Intentionally left blank

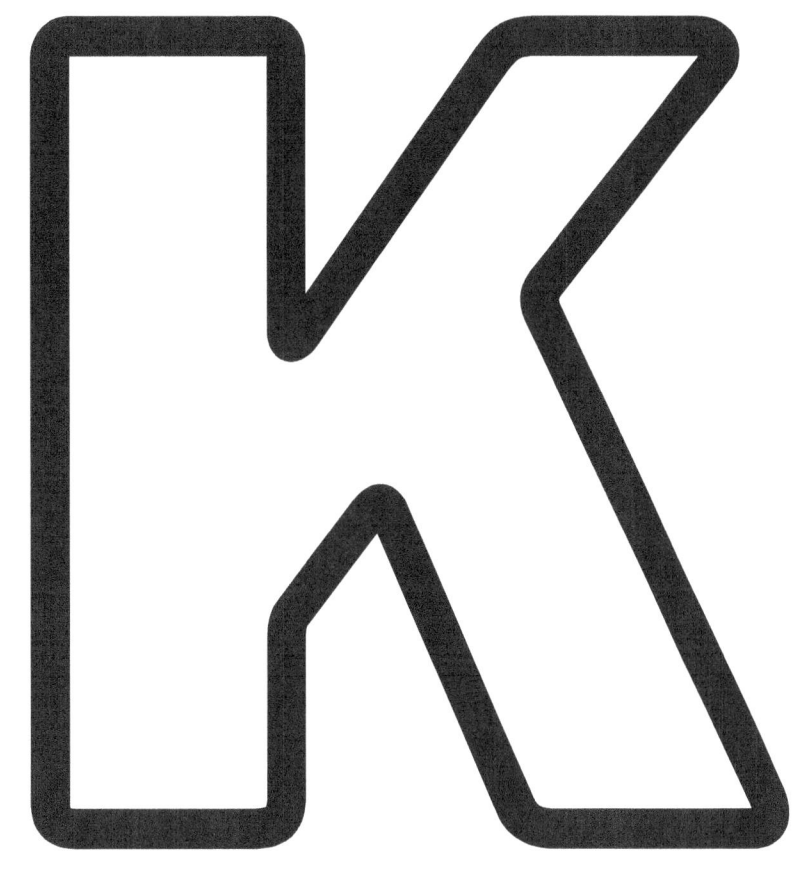

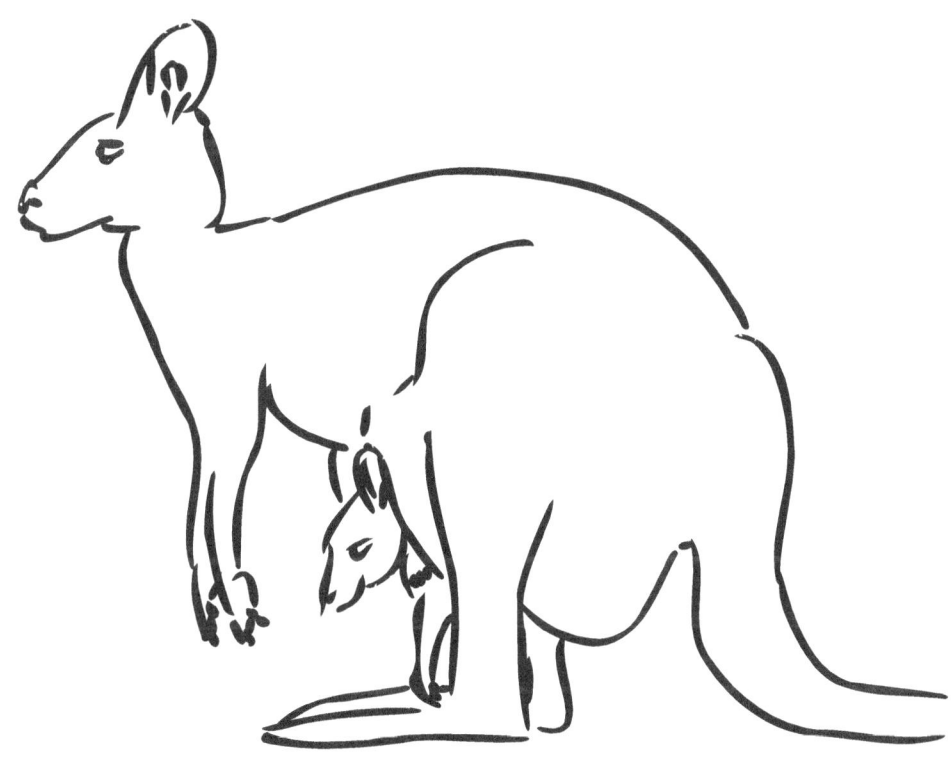

Intentionally left blank

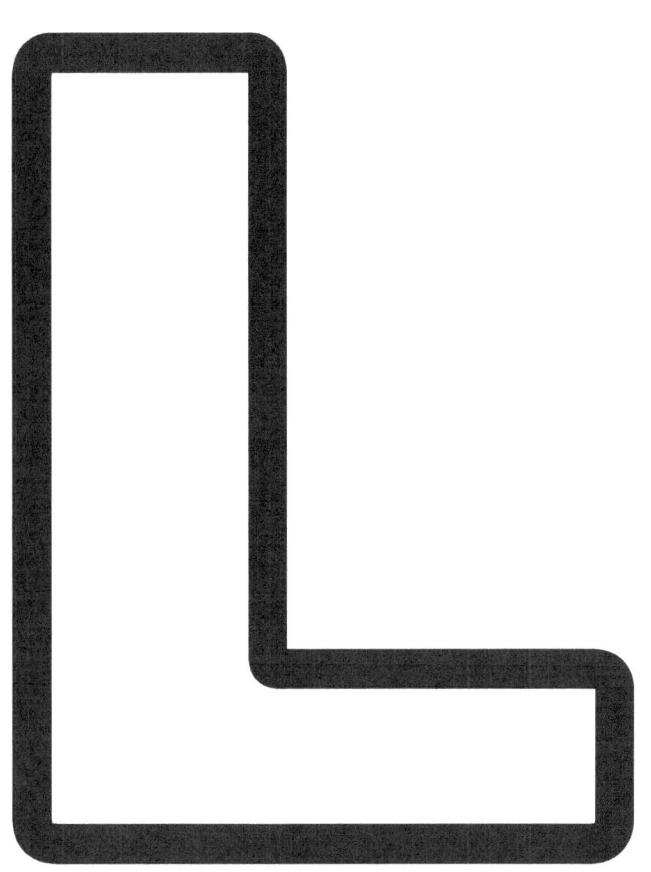

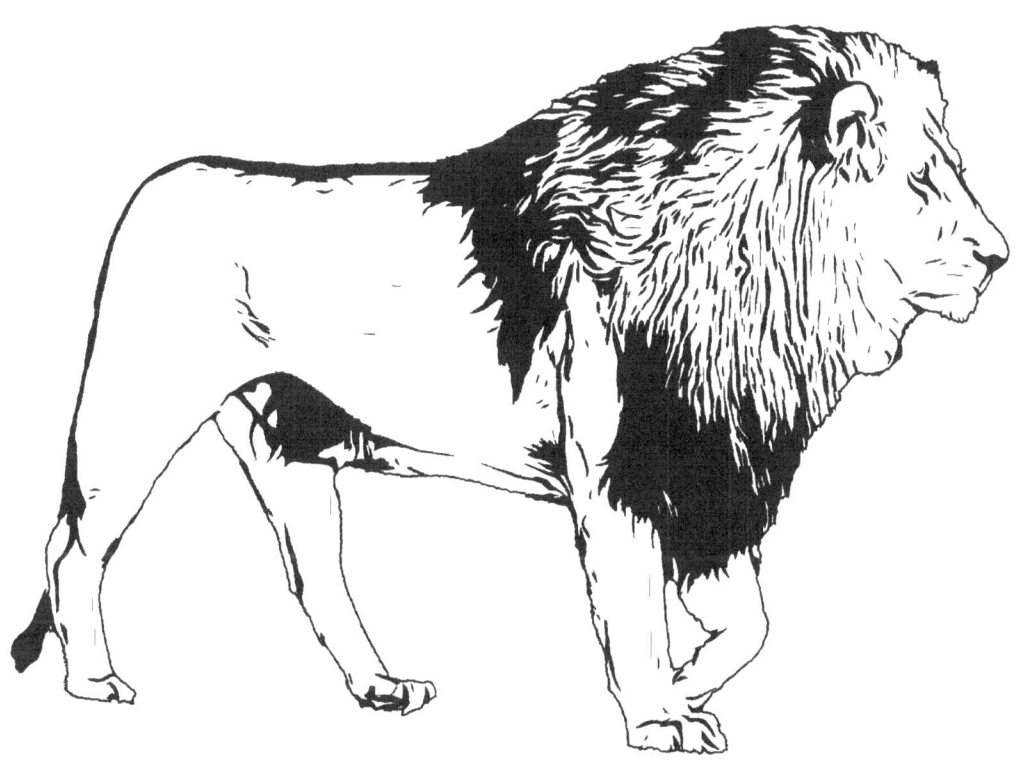

Intentionally left blank

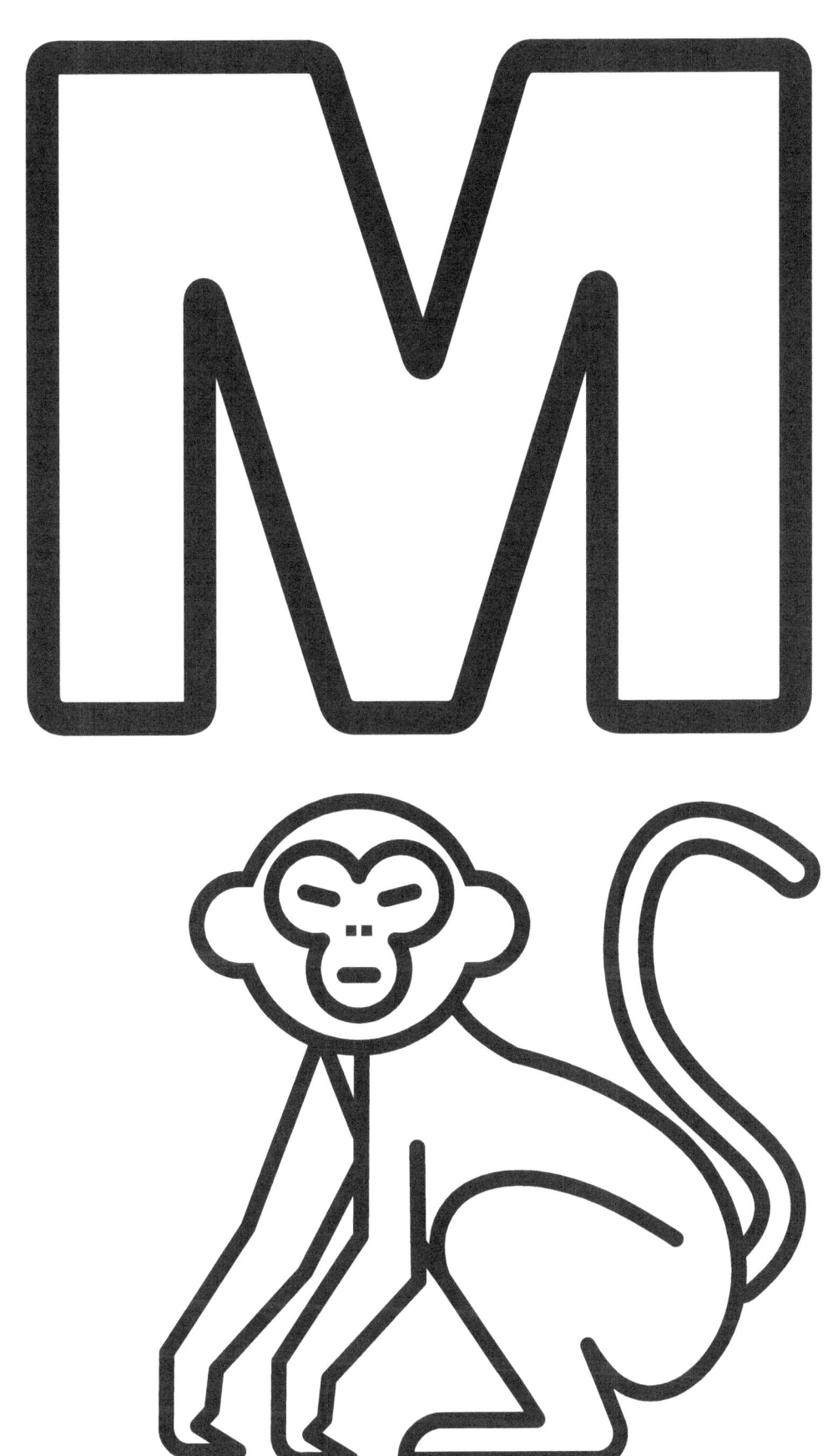

Intentionally left blank

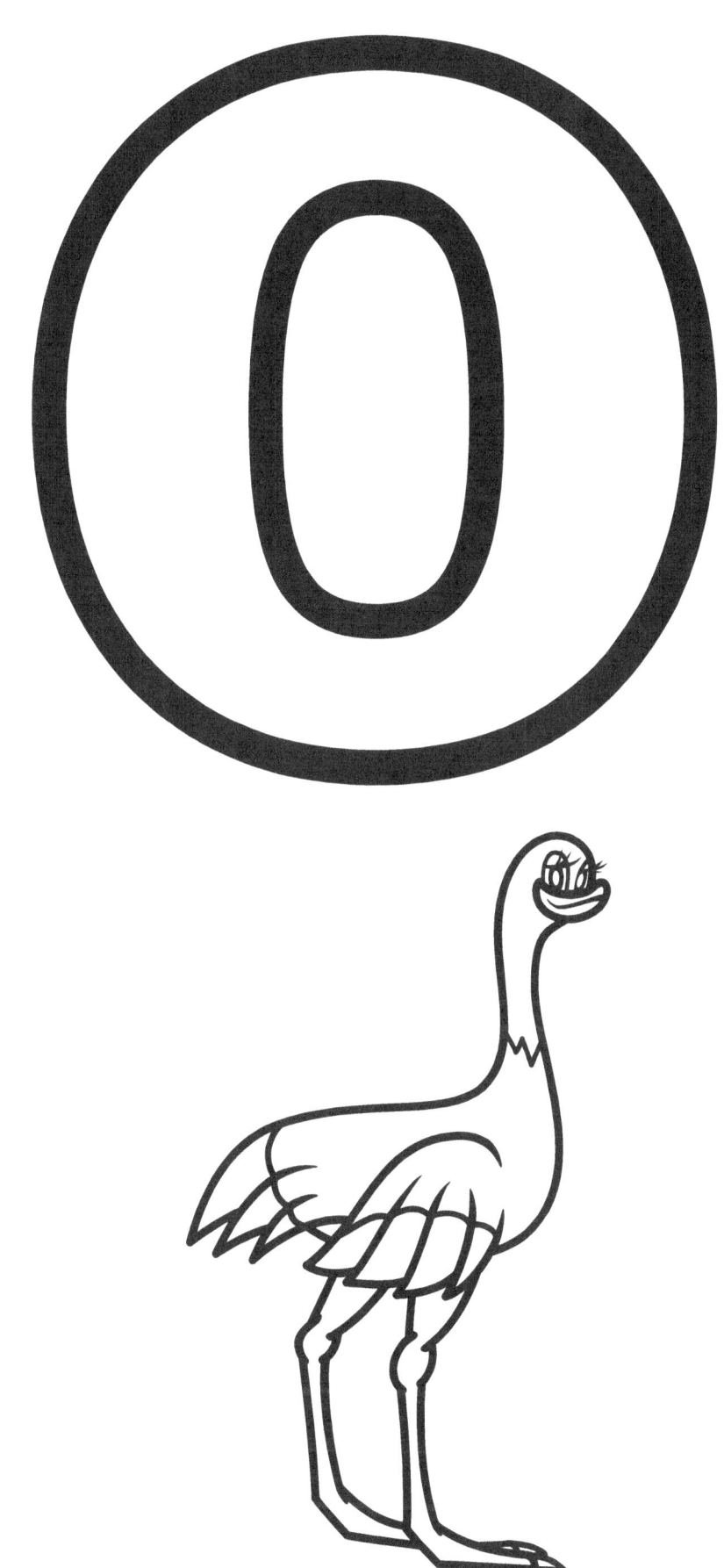

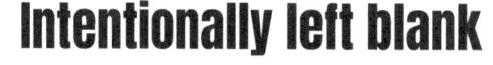
Intentionally left blank

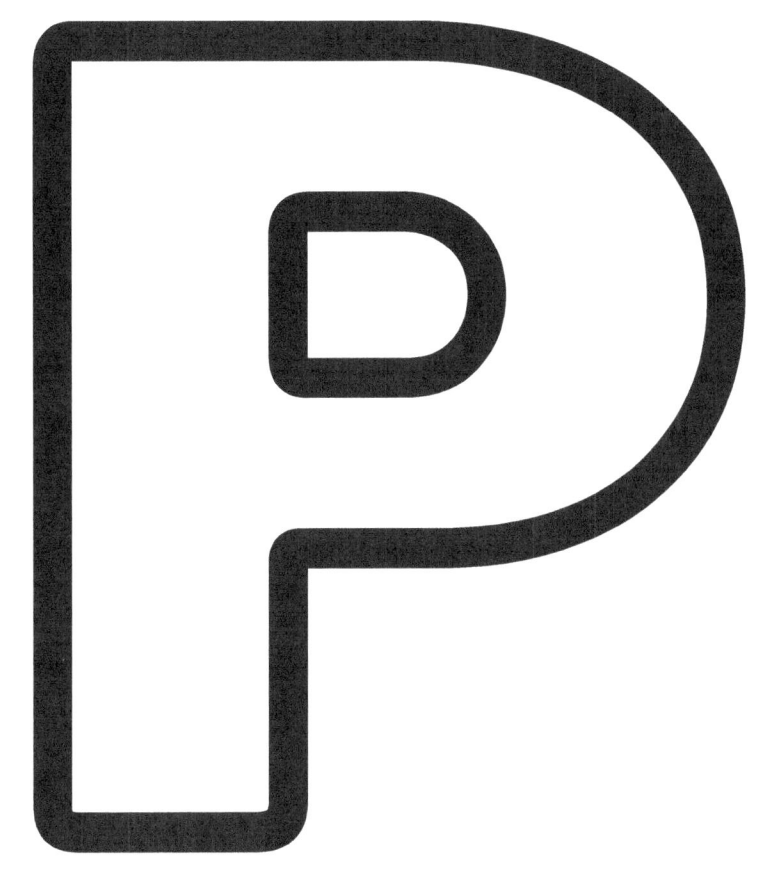

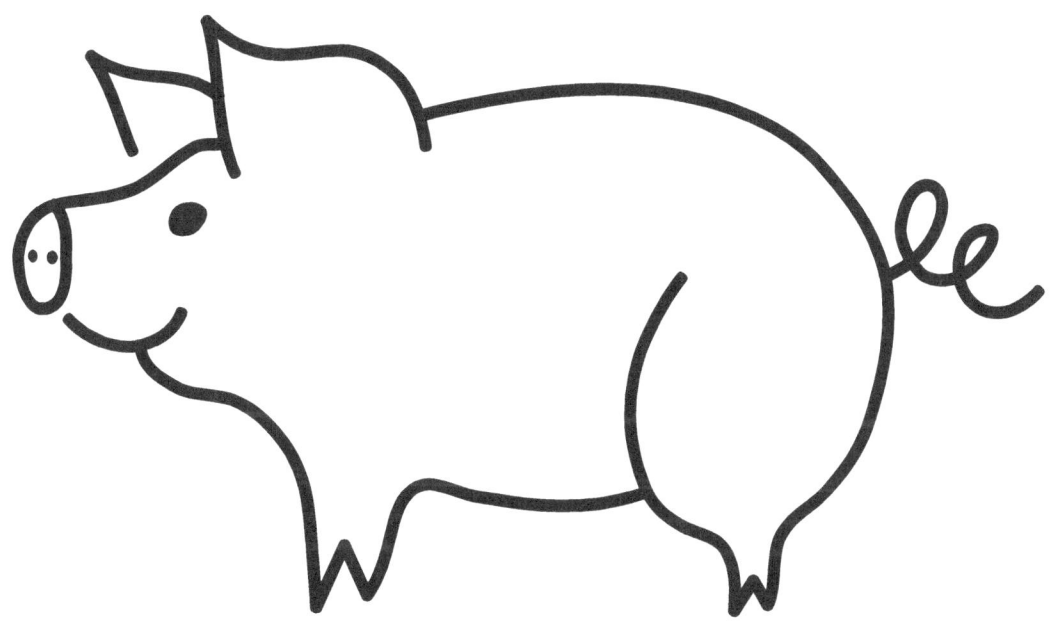

Intentionally left blank

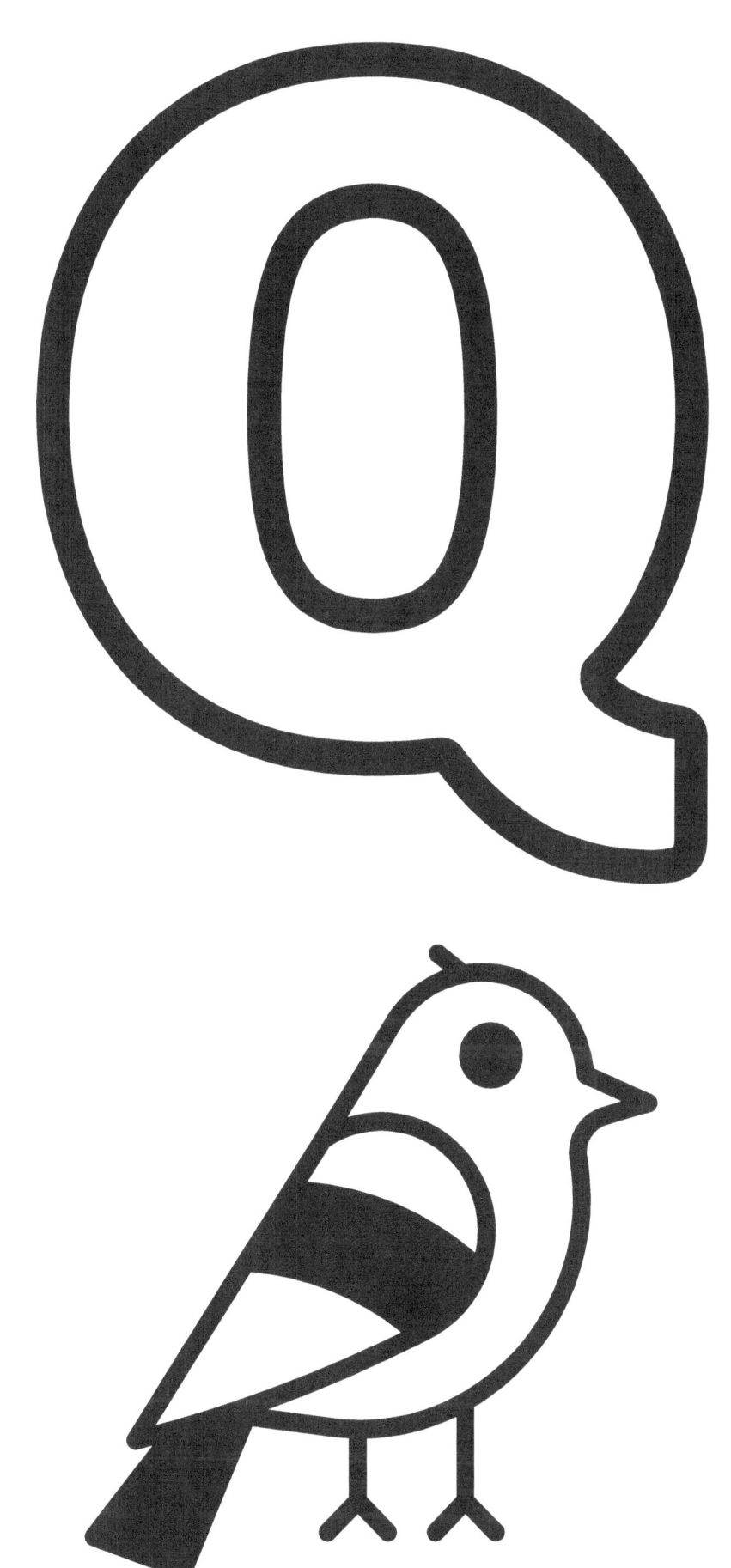

Intentionally left blank

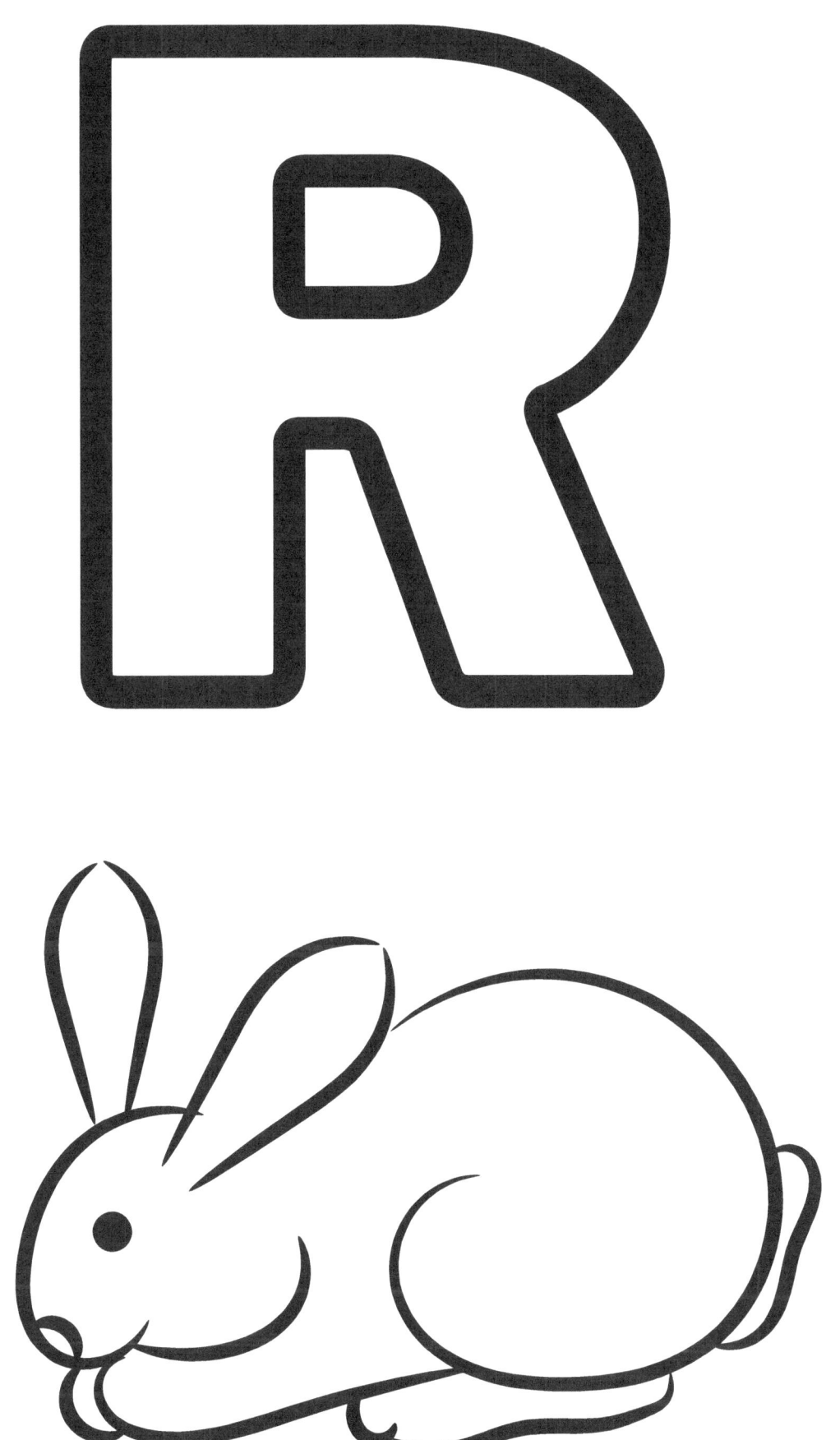

Intentionally left blank

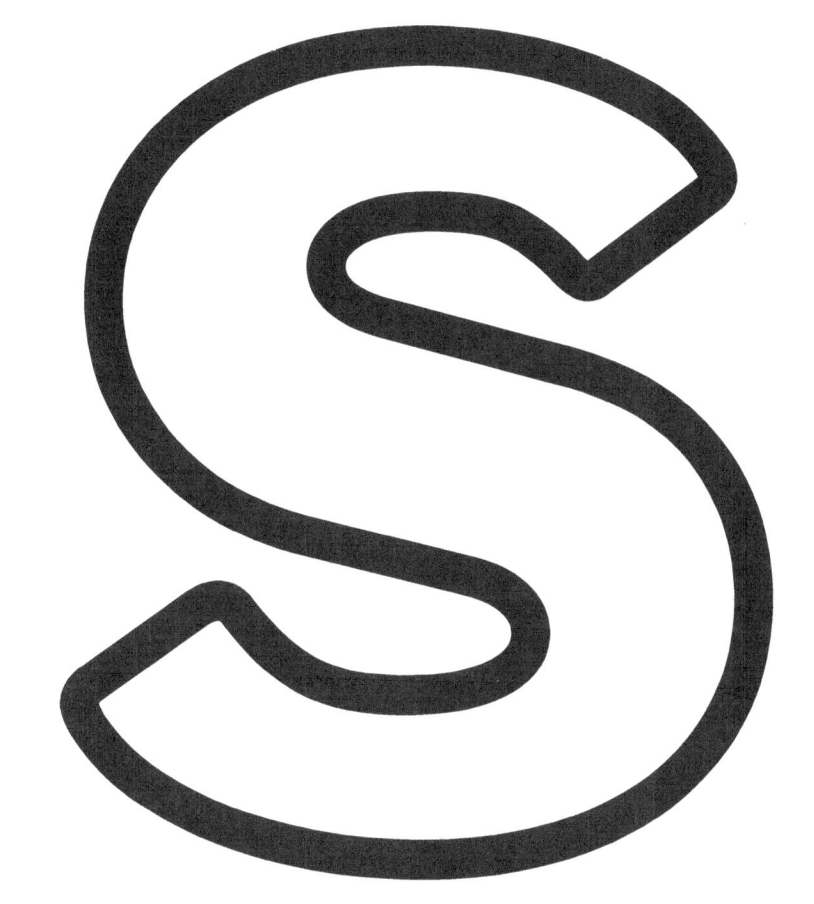

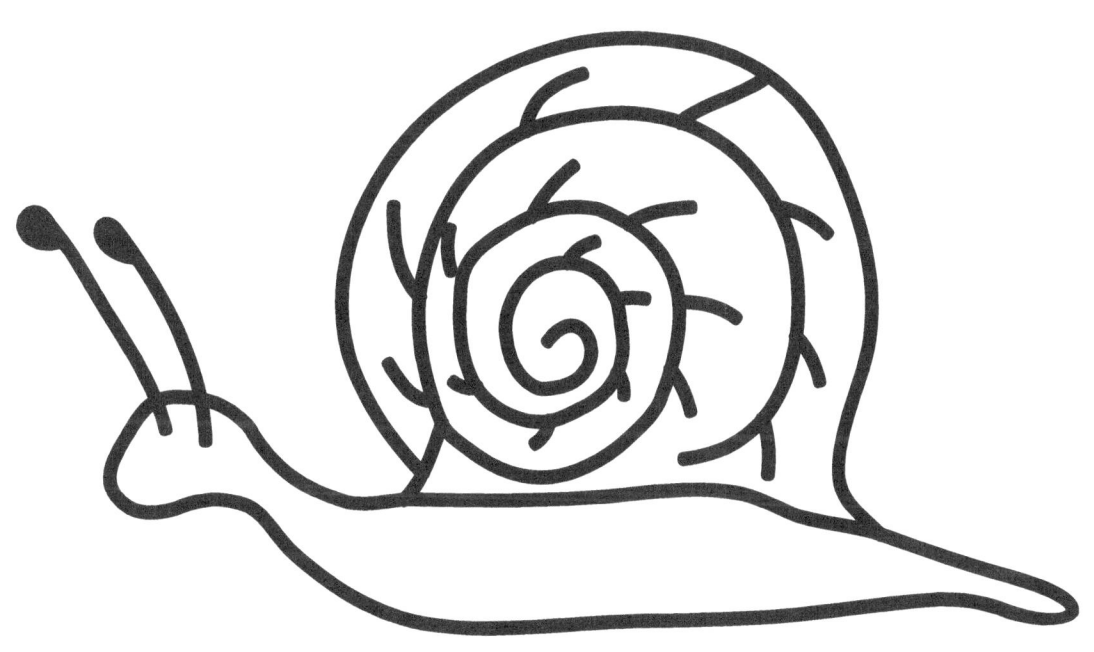

Intentionally left blank

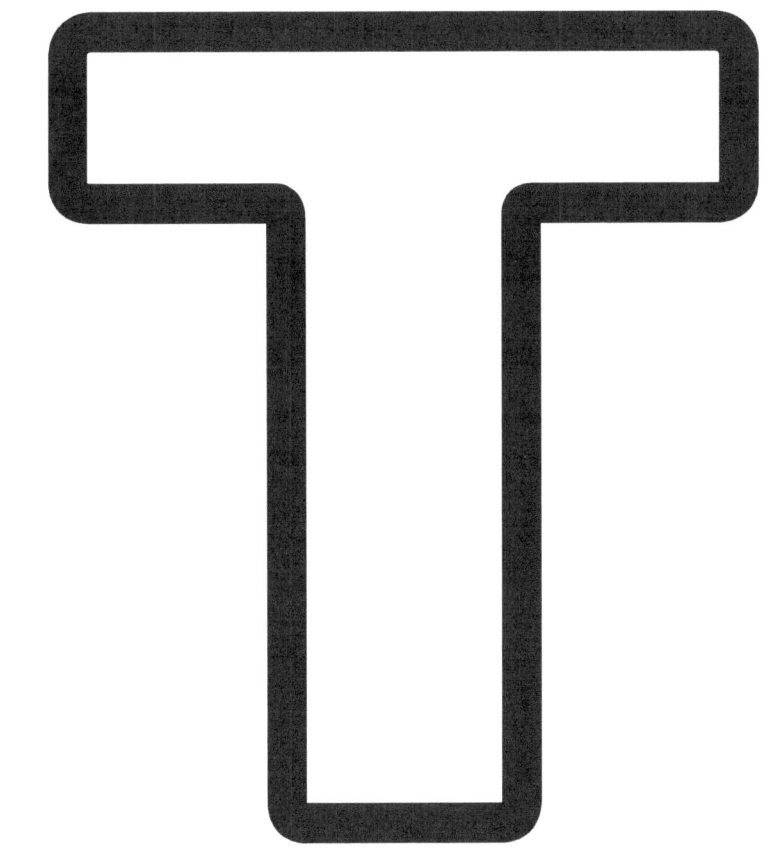

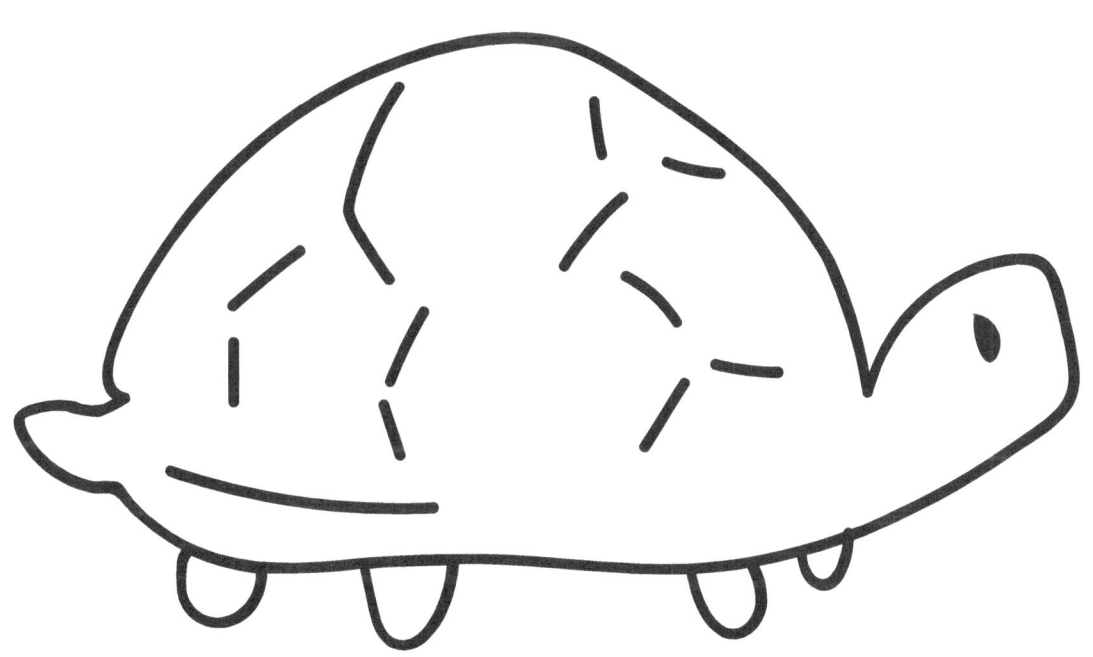

Intentionally left blank

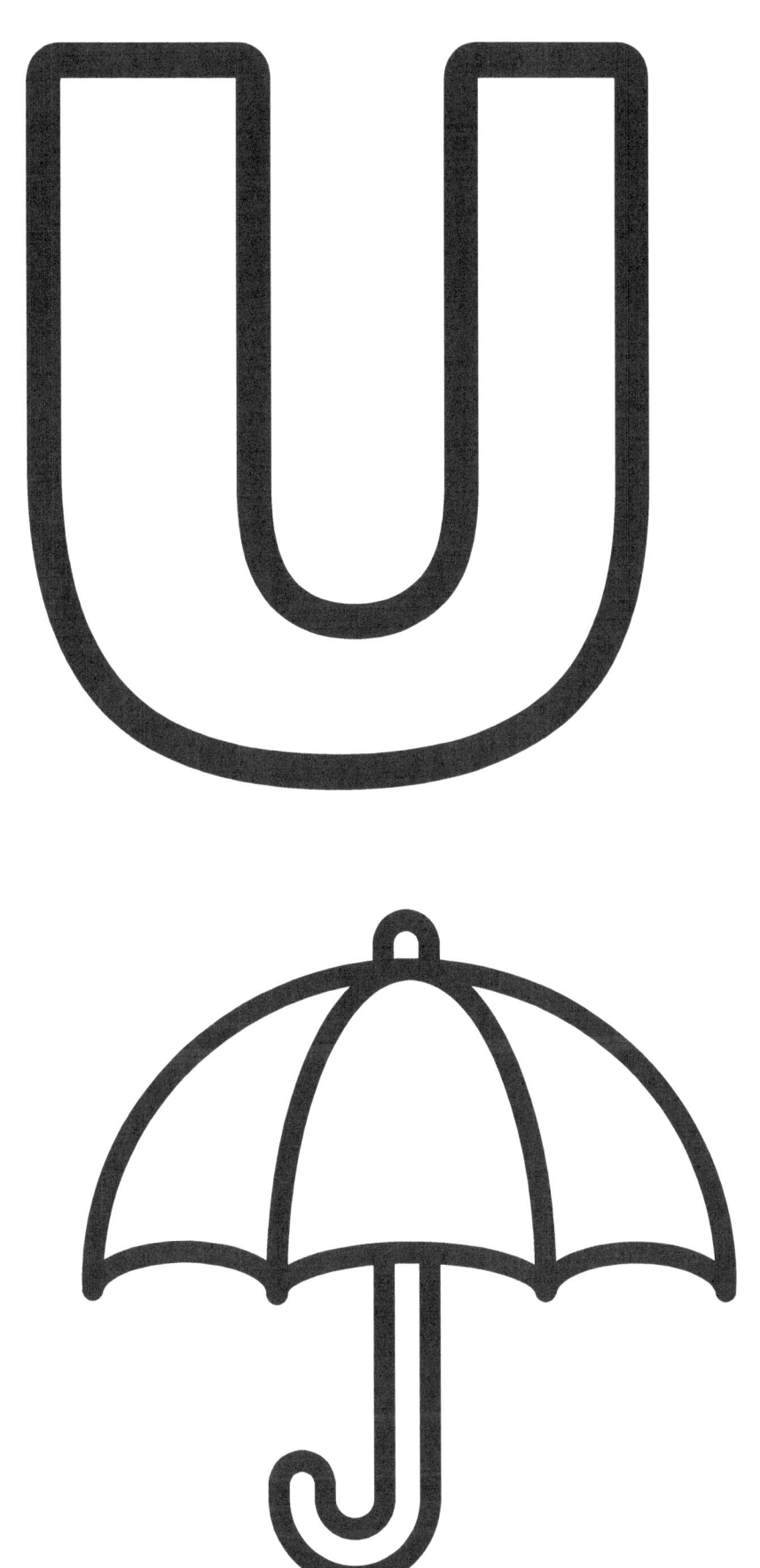

Intentionally left blank

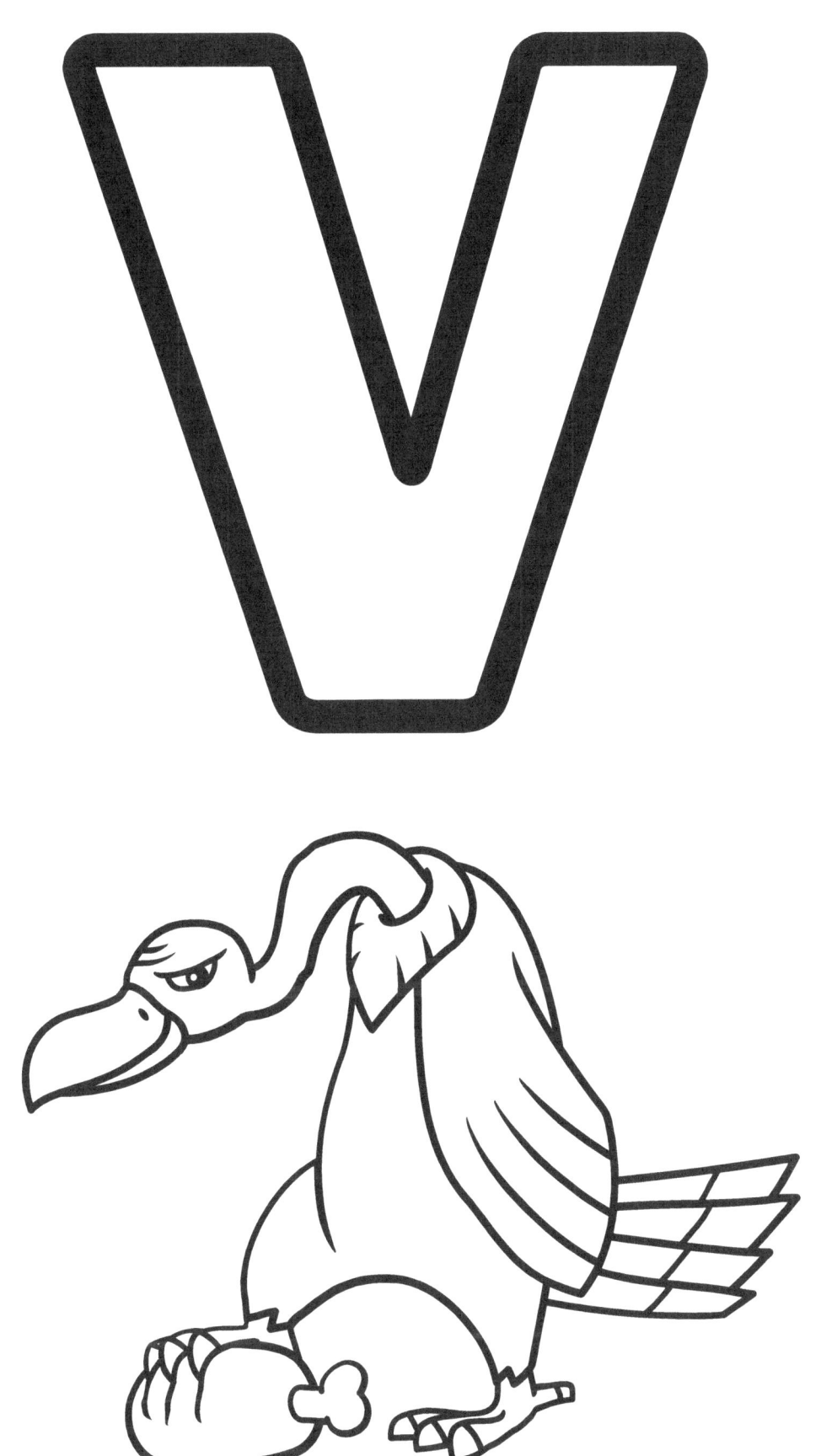

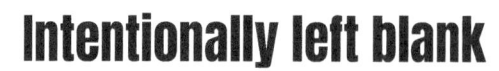
Intentionally left blank

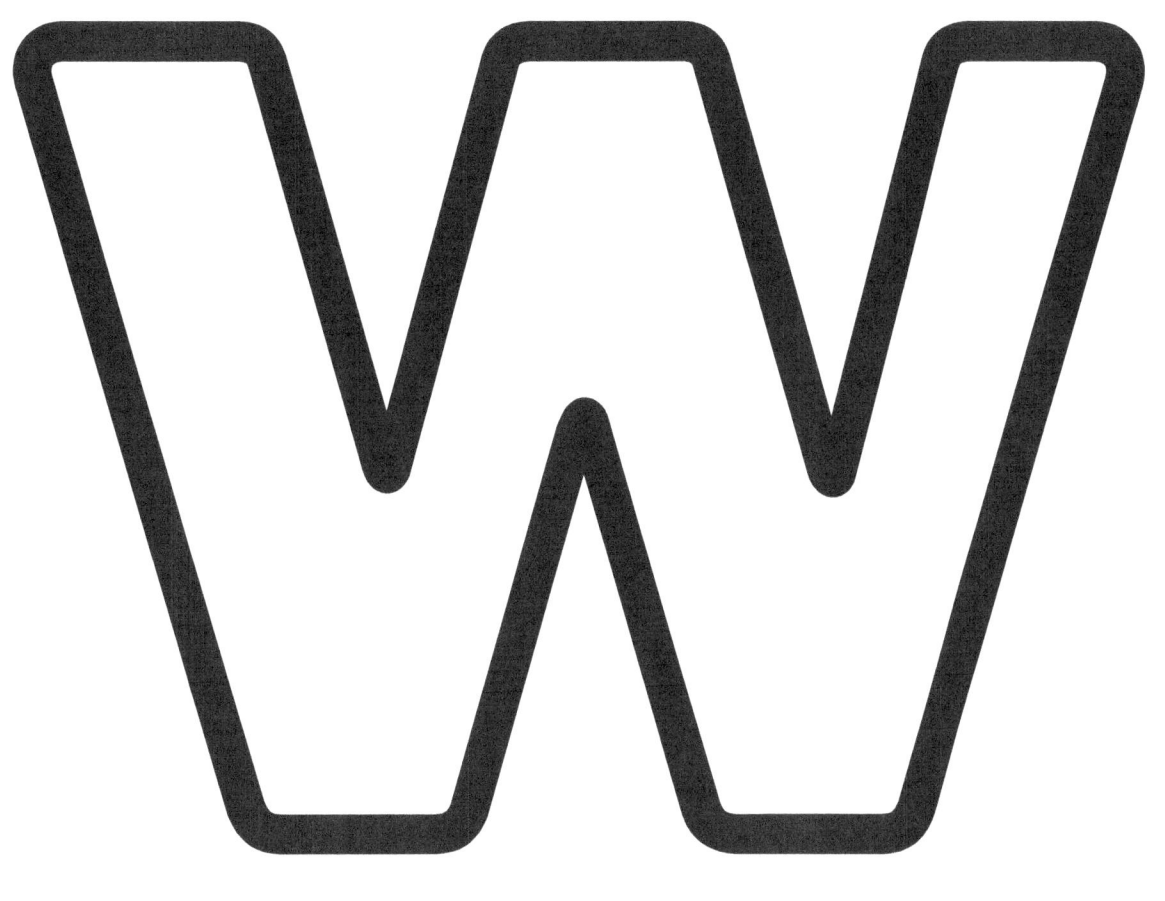

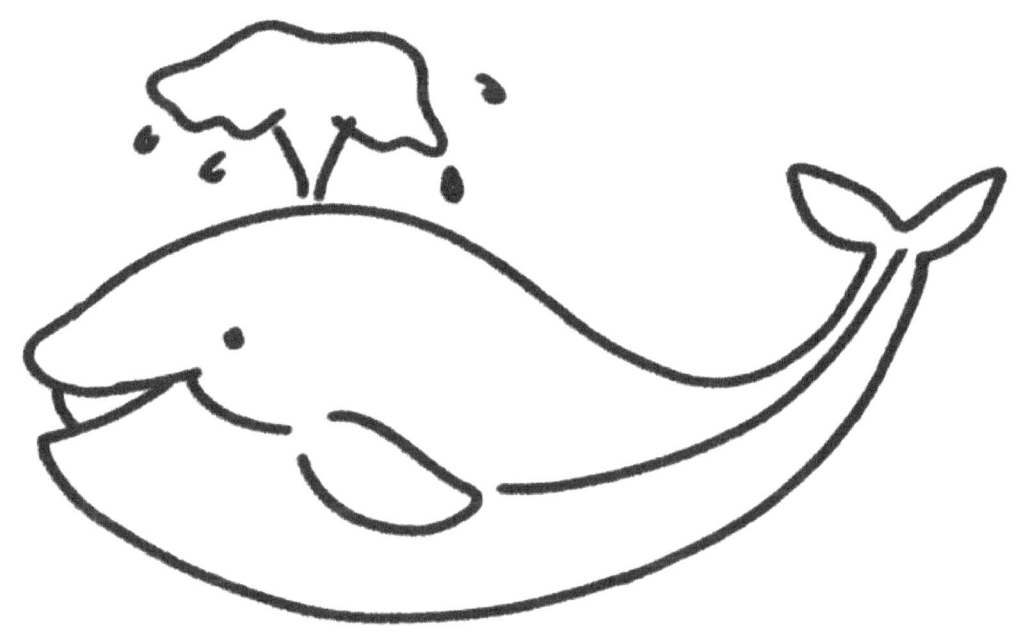

Intentionally left blank

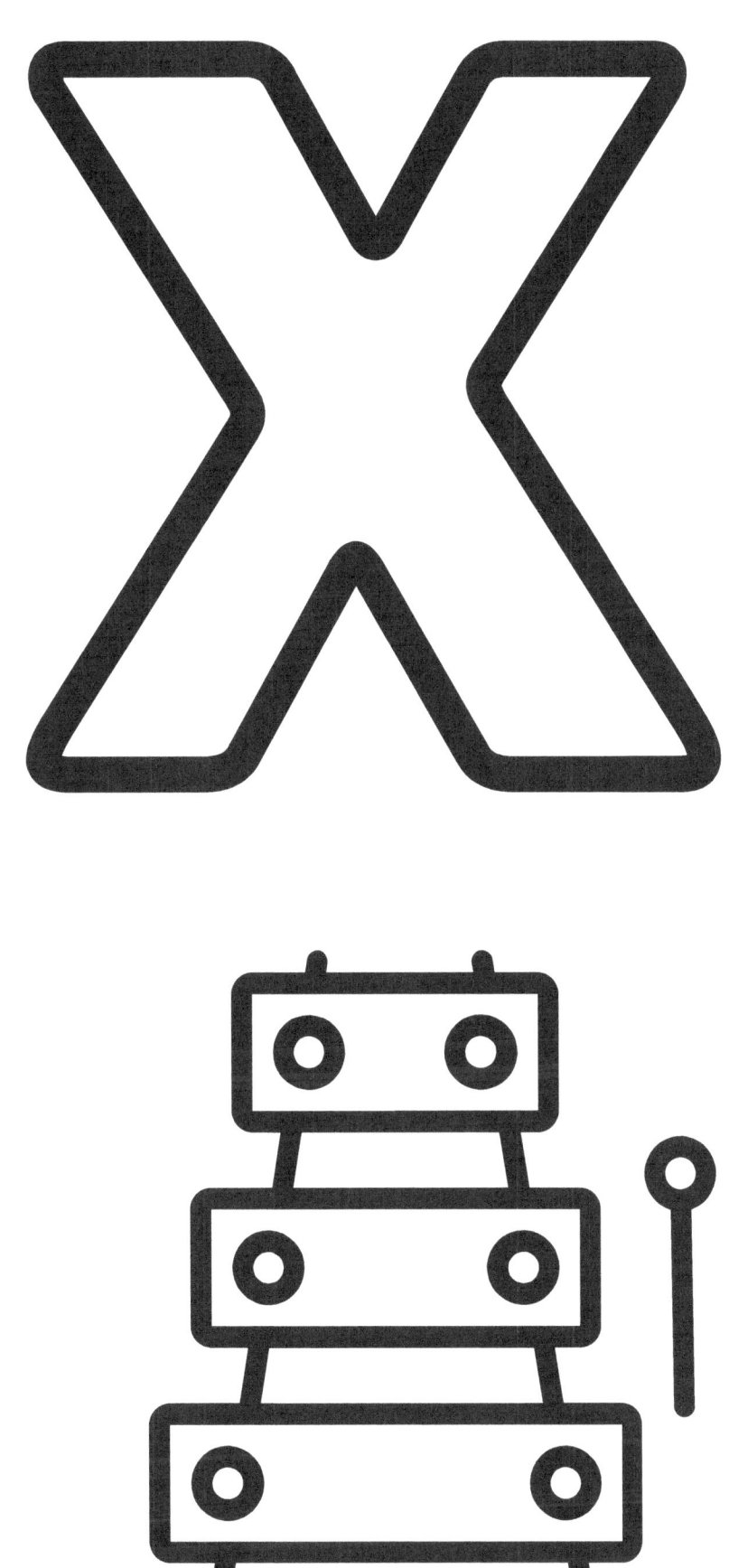

Intentionally left blank

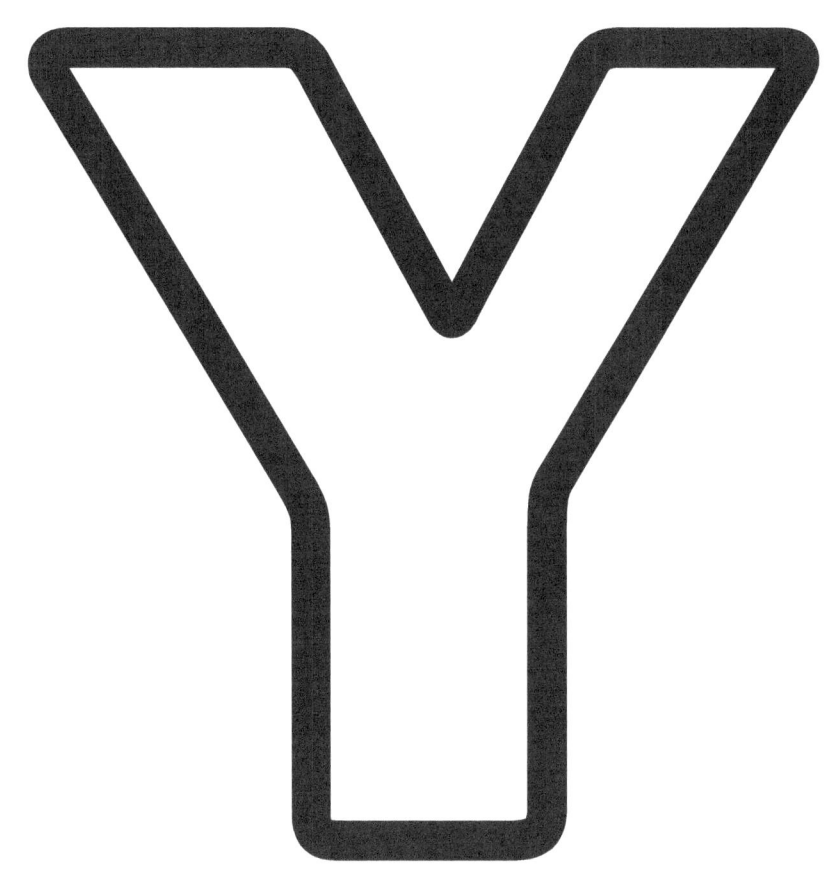

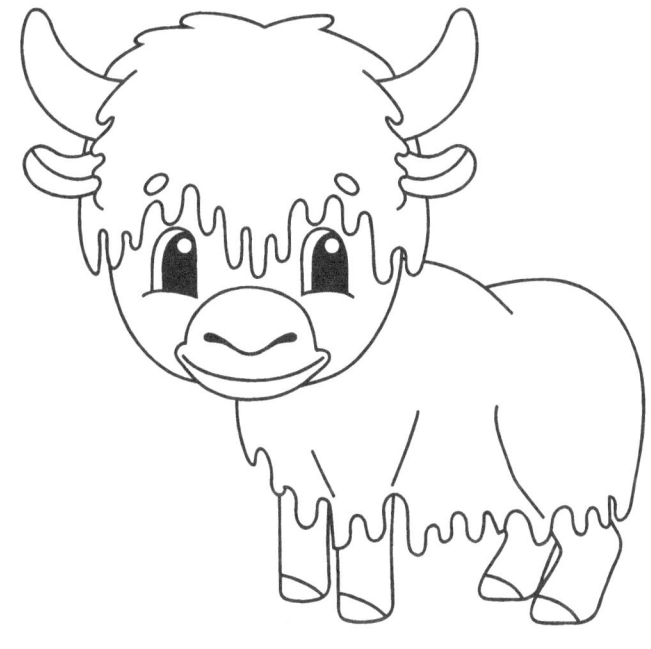

Intentionally left blank

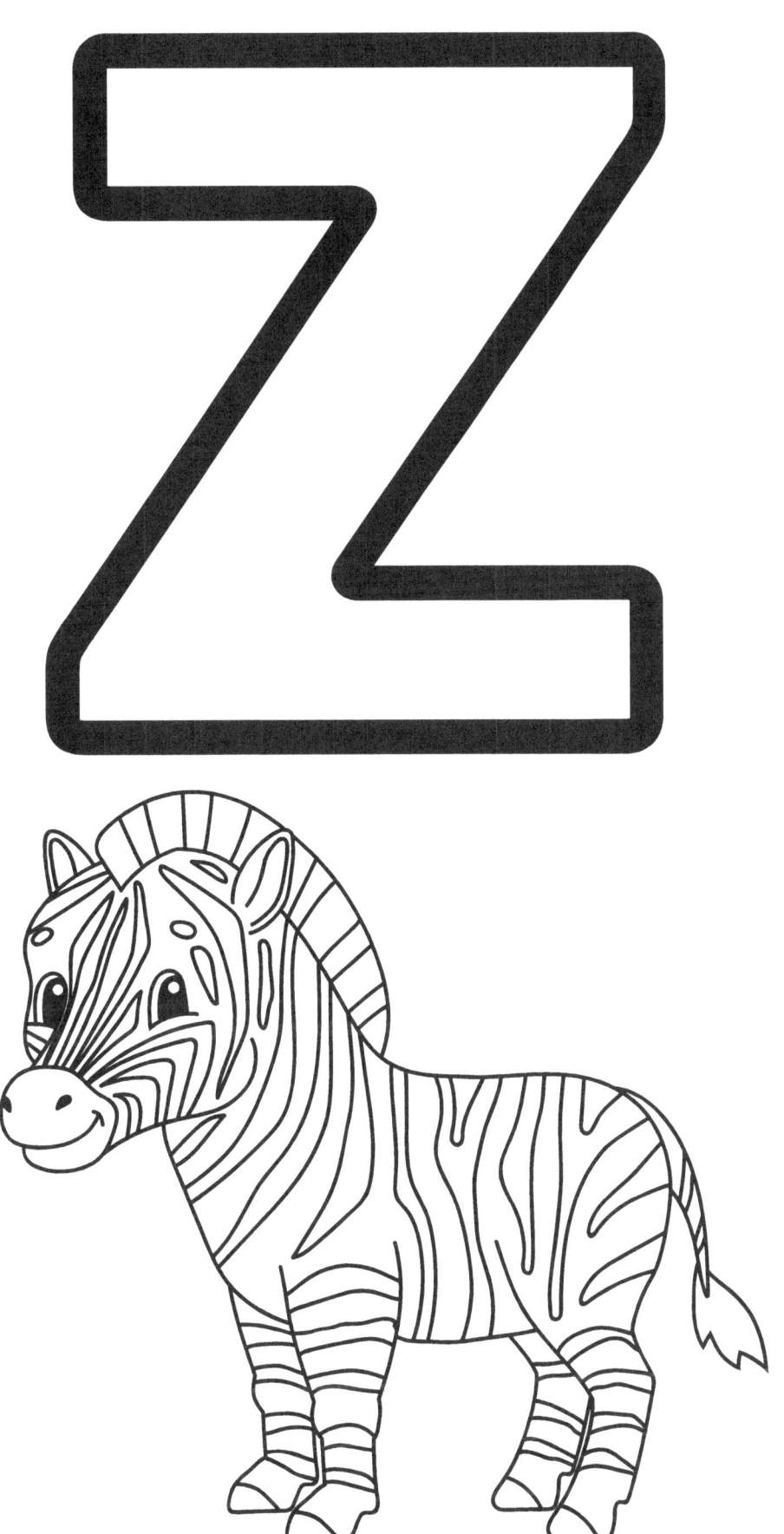

Intentionally left blank